NATURE Kids

The Weta

Text by John Lockyer • Photographs by Rod Morris

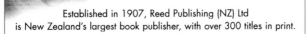

Established in 1907, Reed Publishing (NZ) Ltd
is New Zealand's largest book publisher, with over 300 titles in print.

For details on all these books visit our website:
www.reed.co.nz

Published by Reed Children's Books, an imprint of
Reed Publishing (NZ) Ltd, 39 Rawene Rd, Birkenhead,
Auckland 10. Associated companies, branches and
representatives throughout the world.

ISBN 1 86948 850 4
First published 2000
Reprinted 2002

Edited by Carolyn Lagahetau
Designed by Sharon Whitaker

Printed in New Zealand

Contents

Who, what, where?

There are more than 100 different sorts of weta.

...ta are insects.
...ey have been on Earth since
...osaur times.
...ta live in many countries
...und the world.
...ay, many types of weta are
...dangered.

Giant weta are the largest insects in New Zealand.

They grow as long as 100 millimetres and weigh as much as a small bird.

Family tree

Weta belong to the same group as crickets and grasshoppers. There are five types of weta. They are the giant weta, the tree weta, the ground weta, the tusked weta and the cave weta. Weta live all over New Zealand.

Giant weta

Ground weta

Tusked weta

Tree weta

Cave weta

Good looks

Weta have large heads, long antennae and small mouths.
They have strong jaws.
A hard skeleton covers the outside of their bodies.
They breathe through holes on the sides of their bodies.
Sharp spines are on the back of each hind leg.
Many weta have ears on their front legs.

Weta have
four ears —
two on each
front leg.

Antennae can be
twice as long
as a weta's
body

Feeling and tasting

Weta don't have a nose and they can't see very well.
They use antennae to feel for food.
When weta find food, they always use their palps to taste it first.

Palps are on the weta's jaw. They look like paddles.

Weta always keep their antennae clean.

If a weta breaks an antenna, it will grow a new one.

Dinnertime!

Weta are too slow to catch moving prey.
They eat plants, fruit, leaves and dead insects.
They like both fresh food and rotting food.

Sounds

Weta
make noises
when they
are calling to
other weta and
when they
are angry or
frightened.

Many kinds of weta are noisy
at night.
They make a noise that sounds
like sandpaper rubbing on wood.
To make this noise, they rub their
spiny back legs against the sides
of their bodies.

Cave weta
have no ears
and make no
sounds.

Home, sweet home

During the day, tree weta live in holes in trees.
Ground weta live in old worm and grub holes in the earth.
Tusked weta live in tree holes and ground holes.
Giant weta live under stones and rotting bark.
Cave weta live in caves or damp, dark bush.

Weta are nocturnal; this means they only come out at night.

Weta especially like dark, warm, damp nights.

Ground weta enter their holes tail first.

Tree weta enter their holes head first.

15

Eggs

Female weta lay eggs all through the year.
They lay them under bushes, in soft, damp soil.
Up to six eggs are laid at one time.
The eggs take about one month to hatch.

One weta can lay more than 300 eggs during its life.
The eggs won't hatch unless the soil is warm and damp.
Eggs can stay unhatched for more than four months.

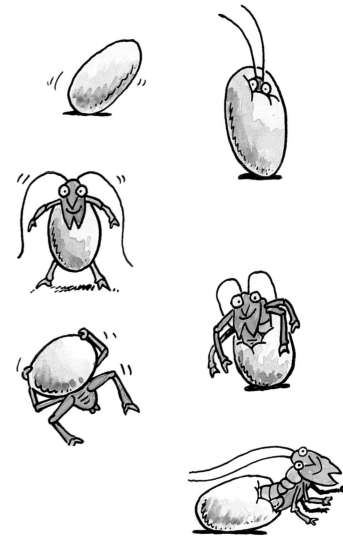

Young ones

After hatching, the tiny, jumping baby
weta scatter among the leaves and bark.
It takes almost eighteen months for weta
to become adults.
Weta moult as they grow bigger.
They live for about two years.

Weta often
eat their old
skins.

This picture is of a male weta just after it has moulted.

When weta moult, they split their skin then wriggle out of it.

Most weta moult nine times during their life.

Danger! Beware!

Although weta look scary, they are harmless.
They have no sting but can bite.
They protect themselves with camouflage
and by kicking their back legs.

Weta sometimes use pincer claws on their front legs to scratch enemies.

Tusked weta
fight with their
long, curved
tusks.

Help save us

Many weta are eaten by cats, rats and tuatara.
Some types of weta have been moved to safe places
like zoos and islands to help them survive.

Weta have
been in
New Zealand for
70 million years.

The weta's body can be divided into three sections:

The head	used for feeding and getting information abouts its surroundings
The middle section	used for movement such as running and climbing
The rear	used for making eggs

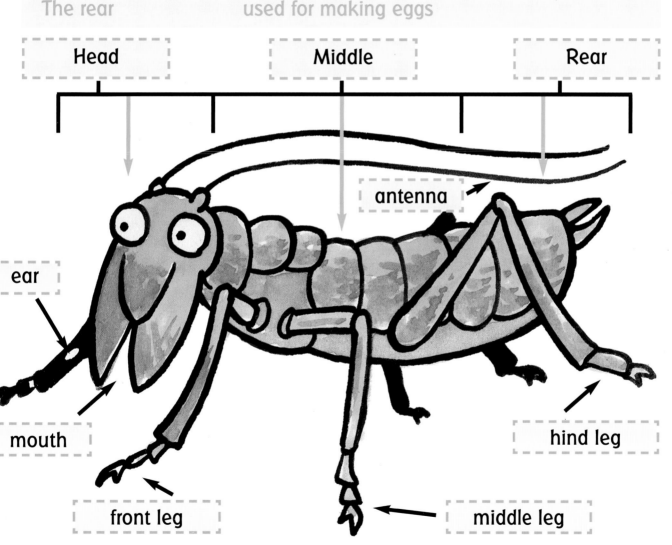

Head

Middle

Rear

antenna

ear

mouth

front leg

middle leg

hind leg

Index